SELF-IMPROVEMENT AND MOTIVATIONAL TIPS FOR SUCCESS

ANTHONY EKANEM

Contents

Preface

We all have formed our definitions of happiness right from childhood. A lot of these perceptions are because of conditioned development, that is, they are a part of our habits due to repetitive inculcation by parents, teachers and society in general. That is why none of us has pondered about what exactly makes us feel happy! This feeling has been left to our sub-conscience and we simply feel happiness according to the situation we are in.

A lot of small things can give happiness to us. For instance, just the thought of shopping or spending money tends to excite us and makes us feel happy. Opportunities and new ideas also have a similar effect on us. This excited state makes us imagine things related to these incidents. For example, the perspective of going on vacation while getting an office bonus would not only make us excited but also make us plan and imagine the holiday. We would feel the bliss without actually being on the vacation itself! However, when being on the actual vacation, the excitement tends to settle down as one begins to feel contented.

The same is the case with objects. We are quite crazy about purchasing the latest cell phone, laptop, I-pod or a new car. But once we own that thing, the excitement settles down and the appeal doesn't stay the same. The cycle of excitement begins again when another new product is launched.

Let's pause for a while and seriously think about our domain of happiness. Is it pertained to acquiring the latest objects only? Does it end with wishes being fulfilled? Is our domain of happiness limited to spending good time with family or friends only? We are so involved in this cycle of wishes that we forget to see what real happiness is and how it can be achieved.

The domain or definition of happiness varies for every individual as they have their individual needs. For some people, achieving a good career path provides happiness. For some, it is their fulfilment of goals and objectives whereas bringing happiness to the face of the deprived can give some people happiness.

However, everybody doesn't have it easy. Our income, education, family, environment, society and friends all affect our domain of happiness. We might not always have the desired income needed to fulfil our wishes or maybe the career isn't going as smoothly as we had planned. So what does it do to us? Does it burst our balloon of hope and excitement or does it renew our hopes, make us clear our visions and set ahead for the future with new motivation? How do you react when things don't turn out as you had planned? Most importantly, is your reaction appropriate or do you need to change your attitude and perception?

This book is all about 'you' and how you can change dimensions to look ahead to a better future. The upcoming chapters are a complete guide so that you can set yourself in a new direction. After all, success is all about having the right paradigm shift!

CHAPTER ONE

Self-Improvement through Motivation

To be happy and satisfied, one needs to be motivated. Motivation gives us the hope to look ahead and dream higher. It is the force that propels us to go ahead. But why do we need to change? People change for various reasons. Some change because they don't want to face the pain in their lives. Some change because they are sick of their failures. For instance, poor grades can make us realize the importance of hard work while studying and can motivate us to change. Similarly, debts can make us look for other jobs or to do more than one job.

The world is full of negativity, and regardless of whatever people say, we need to face this negativity and try to get over it. But it is you who has to decide. Who is in charge of your life? You or your surroundings? Once you decide that you are in charge of whatever happens to you, you will put your foot down and get over whatever negativity surrounds you.

It is easy for us to remain in the shelter of our comfort zone, but have you ever tried stepping out of your comfort zone and taking a sneak peek into what lies beyond? What exactly prevents you from doing so? Failure? Fears? Shame?

The basic thing that you need to improve yourself is first, to have a goal and set some objectives. Once you know where you are headed, you will easily maintain your focus and not be strayed away by anything that hinders you.

Next is to set some concrete plans which can enable you to go for your goals. While planning, don't just think within your comfort zone. Step out of the box to discover a newer you. Identify your problems and limitations and use techniques to get over them. Make sure that you know what your weaknesses are and correct them while being in the domain of the ethical values that you cherish.

Execute your plan and don't worry whether you have succeeded or not. Failures would not break you, but rather would strengthen you. Rework your plans if they fail, identify loopholes and use methods which help you overcome these loopholes. Every failure teaches you what to avoid and ends up giving you a big lesson. Learn from these lessons so that you can strengthen the newer you.

Try to avoid negative thoughts and people. Such thoughts and words tend to self-limit your potential and make you go weak. If you believe in your plans, you focus on your direction and make changes only if you wish to, regardless of what others say. This approach would make you jump over the limitations that block your way.

Lastly, you need to enjoy life and take things as they come. When you are happy and content, your mind would work faster and success will come your way. So hold on hard to your dreams, take control of your life and set ahead to enjoy the journey with a newer you.

Challenging Yourself to be Motivated

The initiative of having a goal-oriented behaviour is also known as Motivation. The actual purpose of motivation is to decrease mental or physical stress and to raise the factor of happiness in a person. Motivation is generally of two types: Intrinsic and Extrinsic. Intrinsic motivation is that which is exhibited by the delight or concern in the given activity and is rather intrinsic, that is, within the individual. On the contrary, extrinsic motivation is that which is exhibited or enhanced by external factors such as money, rewards, gifts or intimidation.

If a person is strongly motivated to achieve or gain something huge, then that person is involved in aiming high for the future. This is the reason why motivation is interlinked with challenges. Moreover, our body, physically and mentally, is designed in such a way that it is always ready to accept and face different challenges.

Motivation can be explained further by one of the scenarios given below:

If, for instance, one comes to know that they are in danger, then their immediate response would be to take all the necessary measures to prevent themselves from danger and ensure safety.

The scenario mentioned above challenges one's security and lifestyle. That is why it manages to raise one's motivation towards the act of protecting themselves. In this manner, we need to engage ourselves in various challenges so that our morale and motivation remain boosted. Facing and overcoming challenges tends to impart a positive feeling that increases one's motivation. It also makes you test your patience and to what extent you can stretch yourself.

The best way to deal with challenges in your lifestyle is to take the daily routine as a challenge and use it to alter your identity and thinking. You can set daily goals and try to accomplish them. A person's general character and personality are formed via learning and practising the norms and values of the societal culture. However, all values do not have a positive influence on us. That is why one has to have a correct frame of mind and motivation so that one can create values and live by them. Therefore, continuous re-conditioning of your inner self would let you see everything as a challenge and undergo the change of values that are needed. Too much relaxing of the brain would make you feel like a laggard so it's better to keep the brain in action.

It might be tiring to keep yourself up to the challenges all the time but when you become used to it, you would master the skill of being motivated and successful.

Being successful is very important for everybody. It is the intrinsic need of human beings to gain recognition, dignity and success. However, to be successful, one needs to be highly motivated. This is so because motivation gives one the power to propel themselves towards success. However, motivation is important for success due to other reasons as well. Some of these are as follows:

1. Motivation serves as the basic start-up:

Have you ever been forced to do some work that you don't like? How have you reacted to that work? Not that positive for sure! Now compare that work to some work that you like to perform. Do you realize the difference in your attitude when you compare both of these tasks? Which one was accomplished quickly with better work quality? Of course, the task you liked performing was performed way better. This is what motivation is. It serves as a startup so that you can get ahead with the work. The most difficult aspect of any task is to get it started, and once things get started, there is no looking back. Therefore, motivation is a key factor in making you get started on your way to success.

2. Motivation makes you keep moving:

When on the path to success, you are not always rewarded with success. One has to fall many times before getting up and moving ahead. Obstacles, after all, are an integral part to make you stronger. It makes you worthy of your success. So, you have to be mentally prepared to face the tough work, the challenges and the problems to move ahead. So, you need to keep yourself motivated to keep pushing and going ahead.

3. Do something extra:

What is it that the successful do that we don't? We have always wondered about this and got no answer. It's what they do 'extra' that makes them successful. Even if you have started up, moved on and faced challenges, you still need to push it beyond what your normal capacity is. Only then would you yield the fruit of success! Doing the necessary would get the job done anyway, so how about doing that extra bit, so that the task itself would boast about who has done it? Think about it!

4. It's boring without motivation:

Why do you take books to read or listen to music when going on a long journey? It is to make you feel fresh throughout the journey. The same is the case with motivation. The road to success is long, boring and tedious, but if you have motivation as your companion, then you need not worry about anything. Difficult times can be conveniently endured by motivation as being motivated ensures that you not only do it the right way but also enjoy yourself as you go ahead.

So always feel motivated, keep your hopes high and look towards a brighter future.

Factors behind motivation in a successful life

We all know what motivation is and how it affects us. But often, despite all the knowledge and awareness, we still get confused by the concept of motivation. So what is it that causes all the confusion? Why do we fail to understand motivation?

Well, the basic function of motivation is quite simple. It is to provide us with happiness and remove pain from our life. This is the fundamental on which all the motivational talks, sessions or books are based. What varies is the kind of happiness and pain that it tends to provide. This makes you read books and take sessions to realize what techniques you ought to do to be motivated.

So why exactly is 'motivation' the key factor behind our success? Why not 'intelligence' or 'hard work' for instance? Surely, motivation must have something that it got this status. The real thing is that whenever we want to perform a task, accomplish a goal or simply do some work, we need a certain propelling factor that would make us do that work. This 'propelling factor' is motivation. It is this motivation that tends to make us fulfil our accomplishments and perform some work.

Now the question is: how does our mind feel motivated to make us perform that task? There are three important factors through which our mind functions. These are:
1) Conceptual
2) Perceptual
3) Emotional

These three factors, when functioning together, propel us to do the task. The conceptual factor is responsible to form certain beliefs and reasons. All the motivations we feel arise in this region as once we form a belief about accomplishing something, we feel motivated towards that task. The perceptual region is involved with the collection of sensory data. Once motivated, we use this perceptual sense to relate to our motivation and further increase it. The emotional region is involved with our emotions, which may be fear, happiness, excitement, apprehension or anything related to the task at hand. Motivation is also felt by the emotional region which then gives rise to the elements of excitement and happiness, which we feel when we are motivated.

This cycle of brain functioning tells us how our beliefs and values control our motivation. Once we have set the right approach and geared up with the right beliefs, we would never go astray from our motivated goal. A general rule regarding the formation of beliefs is that one should always look for positive things and find positive beliefs. Positivity is a great supporter of motivation and happiness and it multiplies the effect of motivation. Therefore, if our beliefs are backed up by the foundation of positivity, then we would be able to firmly uphold our motivation.

To conclude, motivation is an asset that is conditioned by our brains. It is in our control how we condition our minds to be motivated. Therefore, have healthy and positive beliefs which can generate and make you feel motivated.

CHAPTER TWO

Goal setting

Goal setting is an important aspect for anyone to be successful. Goal setting enables you to achieve your tasks in an organized fashion and within a limited time frame. Therefore, goals must be set very carefully. Proper planning is needed for goal setting otherwise one can lose focus and get sidetracked. When you have set your goals, you would not only feel confident about the work you are doing, but you would also prioritize what needs are to be fulfilled first. These raise your motivation and self-esteem and you have a positive outlook towards the work that you are doing.

While setting goals or even planning for them, you have to make sure that your goals are SMART. That means, they should be:

1. Specific – i.e. to the point
2. Measurable – i.e. you can judge how much of the goal is accomplished
3. Attainable – i.e. they should be within your potential achievement
4. Realistic – i.e. they should be practically achievable and not something vague
5. Timely – i.e. there should be a time frame in which these goals should be achieved

So, having a SMART approach while setting goals would make you identify the loopholes, gauge yourself and help you achieve your goals easily. These goals would help you climb the ladder of success in slow but concrete steps.

When you have a large goal to achieve, make sure that you divide it into smaller goals which seem easy to achieve. For instance, if you have to submit an important report within a deadline, set smaller goals which would help you achieve your larger goals. In this case, steps such as hypothesis, data collection, result analysis and compilation can be the smaller steps which would help to achieve the goal of report submission. Deadlines should always be associated with smaller goals too so that as you cross them, you are aware of your progress and the work done.

The major part of goal setting is that it should not be rigid. Goals should be set such that they are attainable and flexible. Flexibility doesn't mean being very lenient with the goals, but rather, you should perk up your goal plan as you go along with it. Perking it up would make you correct the problems which you face in the implementation of your goal plan. So, time your goals well, perk them up regularly and plan them according to your priorities so that you don't end up losing the game.

There are many types of goals that you can set such as professional goals, creative goals, personal goals, family goals, educational goals, financial goals and so on. By categorizing your lifetime goals, you would be able to make sure that nothing is left out. Line up your goals so that you know what to prioritize first and when to execute them.

Goal setting not only helps you plan your life, but it also enables you to ensure that you are in control of your life. Setting smart goals this way ensures their timely completion as well as reduces your stress levels.

The distinction between Goals and Values

You might find it interesting to know that everyone in the world is administered by values. Our values and beliefs are reflected through the decisions we make to lead our lives effectively. We adopt certain values from our family, sometimes society or at times we just have them within us. Positive values can be adopted at any pace of life. Make sure the value to pursue has a positive, strong and integral effect on your life. Since you move within a society, it's necessary to espouse such values that meet the demands of society.

Before any other discussion, you need to know the difference between values and goals. Values are not goals; however, they are interrelated with goals and are highly dependent on them. Goals reflect targets whereas positive values form the base of a successful life. You need some basis to lead your life, some beliefs and deeds that drive and support the purpose of your decisions. Effective values always influence your decisions positively and help you choose the right path to success.

While dealing with our clients, we make sure he is aware of the effectiveness of positive values and is highly articulated with them. Jotting down the values is a good way to preserve them in our lives.

Thinking for ways to kill your time on bright sunny days, writing about right and wrong decisions you have made in your past, considering the aspects of excitement and motivation in your life or pondering about the actions that may add stability, provides you edges to realize what actuality values possess in your life. Moreover, you will be clear to differentiate between positive and negative values that influence your life.

You further need to know that your jotting of values should be in the present tense rather than in past for instance write "I am stable financially" more willingly than "I will be stable financially".

All you need is to classify your values and jot them down according to your priority. While writing I am stable financially, you can add other values like "I pay my liabilities on time, at the end of the month I can save some amount and I review my insurance regularly"

You can state your values in the areas of family, friends, community, morals, education, career, health, finances and recreation. Jotting your values and further classifying them might take time but once you are through this course, you will surely be clear about what your values are and how they influence your actions.

Don't hesitate in giving time to identify your values since they are the basis on which you set up your goals. You become clear on what values have influenced your life positively and negatively as well. At times when you are in a state of making a lifetime decision, you need a clear vision of your potential. You already have your values there in your mind but writing them down on a piece of paper will surely help you classify them and set your priorities accordingly.

CHAPTER THREE

Qualities for a Successful Life

We often wonder how a person can be so successful in life! Is it because he inherited the success or is it because of his unique character? There are certain traits that we can adopt to be successful in life. These are:

1. **Sincerity:** Being sincere and following your values and beliefs would guarantee you success. So don't try to be something that you are not. Just be yourself.
2. **Be genuine:** Your actions are greater than your words. So don't exaggerate or deceive others. Just be genuine.
3. **Being wholehearted:** You should be enthusiastic about the things you do. So you should wholeheartedly devote yourself to doing good to others and your community.
4. **Honesty:** Being honest is quite difficult but when you let honesty guide you, you'll achieve greater success. So never deceive or do fraud to get ahead in life.
5. **Heartfelt:** Be honest and appreciate others. Thank people who do good to you and reach out to those in need.
6. **Heartiness:** Be warm and genuine with others. This would radiate your character and affection towards

others.

7. **Humility:** No matter how rich or successful you are, always be humble with others. This would have a longer impact on others.

8. **Personal integrity:** It is important that no matter how successful you become, you should always keep your values intact. Never trade your moral values for material benefits.

9. **Incorruptibility:** Be affirmative and hold your ground to stick towards your beliefs. Don't let others corrupt you.

10. **Good judgment:** Show good and fair judgment in life. Treat everybody with equality and respect.

11. **Focused:** Always maintain your focus and give your total attention to the people you interact with.

12. **Courtesy:** Be good to others and show courtesy even to those who are strangers.

13. **Civic sense:** Exhibit civility and respect. Don't dominate people and speak with kindness and respect.

14. **Wisdom:** Wisdom is gained by experience. Be in touch with your inner self to gain a higher understanding and wisdom.

15. **Charity:** Be generous and charitable to others. Extend help even to those who have not helped you.

16. **Empathy:** Know that everybody is different and has different needs. Understand others' feelings and thoughts.

17. **Sympathy:** Always be sympathetic to people under emotional stress. Try to understand things from their viewpoint.

18. **Compassionate:** Reach out and help those who are in distress. You wouldn't believe the good wishes they'll send out to you.

19. Altruism: Think for others without being selfish. Do good and don't expect things in return. Moreover, don't express to others the favours you do to them.

20. **High-minded:** Give your money, time and knowledge to others so that they can learn from your experience. Don't stop short thinking that they'll get ahead of you. It takes a high mind and a generous heart to do that!

The traits given above are some of the qualities that a successful person should possess. Try to adopt them in daily life and make them a part of your character.

Time Management

In this fast-paced world, a common complaint that almost everybody has is that they lack time to do things. In the past, time management was considered to be a thing that pertained to businessmen only. However, nowadays, everybody falls under the domain of time management. Personal lives, as well as work lives, are well organized once a person follows the domains of time management. Time management benefits one's mental and physical health and gives one a sheer sense of control and satisfaction. People who are in control of their time tend to lead fulfilled and successful lives.

The techniques of time management are not fixed or rigid. Moreover, not all people need to get used to all the time management techniques. That is why one has to look for the technique that best suits them so that the effectiveness is maximum. We all tend to practice time management in some way or the other. What needs to be focused on is how to maximize the effectiveness of our methods.

Some tips for time management are given as follows:

1. Set your goals and objectives. This means that whenever you set out to do something, you should know what purpose you have to fulfil. This would not only give you a sense of direction but would also help you allot specific timings to whatever tasks you have to accomplish.

2. Set clear priorities in your mind. You should know what is more important to you and what needs to be done urgently. Prioritizing would help you assess your needs and requirements in the long term. The ultimate success of a person depends on how well he or she prioritizes things in life. Short-term as well as long-term priorities should be made which should be related to each other. This will eventually make you successful.

3. While prioritizing, be stern with those aspects of your time which are not contributing to the long-term goals that you have set for yourself. Remove those useless areas from your time zone so that you can focus your energies towards achieving more.

4. While mapping your time needs, make sure to include family time and relaxation time in your routine. This would ensure good health and peace of mind. Also, allot time for proper meals and exercise to maintain a healthy normal life.

5. Write down your priorities for a particular period so that you can examine your weaker areas and reinforce the time spent on them.

6. Always keep a diary to plan every day, week and month. A lot of online planners, software, etc., are now available so that you can access your routine plans from home or work without carrying all that load. Using the

conventional diary is better as it lets you get off the computer for a bit and think of your priorities with a peaceful mind. You can start with baby steps and make a To-Do list daily when you start your day. This can slowly enhance your habit of planning your daily routine while you gear up gradually for the full daily time planner mode.

Time management is surely a more satisfying way to lead your life. This also helps you be in control of what you do and reduces stress while improving health.

Stress Management

Stress is the extra tension that we take which causes us to undergo numerous health problems – both physiological and psychological. Thus, it is important to alleviate stress as much as possible.

Stress management is therefore the relief of stress that is important for everyone to know. A lot of factors can cause stress and in stress management, the elimination of these triggering factors is as important as other factors. A lot of research is being carried out in the domains of stress so that more analysis regarding stress management can be done.

Stress has a huge impact on physical health. It can cause cardiac problems, tension headaches, weight loss or even weight gain. There is no reliable outcome of stress on a person as different people react differently to it. In some cases, it can become quite fatal as it can even cause cardiac attacks or strokes.

Human beings are creatures of extreme variance. Therefore, their reactions to stress management also vary to a great extent. All the methods for stress management might not be equally effective for all human beings. That is why one has to discover tools for alleviating stress. Firstly, the cause of underlying stress should be evaluated. Stress can be related to work pressure, family pressure or any underlying health problem over which one has little control. Spouses, children or work peers can be the ones who trigger the stress one faces. Work issues such as stringent deadlines, increased workload, annoying boss, gibbering workmates or a low salary can all enhance your stress levels. Thus one has to discover their stress-causing factor or multiple factors to be able to control stress. It is acceptable that many times, situations are not under your control but just knowing what factors cause you to get stressed can make a huge impact on what modality you choose to alleviate it.

It is said that laughter is the best treatment for any disease. However, one cannot laugh all the time while in stress. That is why effective methods of stress management should be devised. Some people get pets which help them alleviate stress. Some install water fountains or aquariums in their home to make the environment stress-free. Some even use scream therapy, squeezing soft items, going jogging or running, or taking up some hobby so that they can effectively reduce and manage stress.

Vigorous physical activities also tend to decrease adrenaline which can decrease stress levels found in a person. The last management method to alleviate stress is the use of medications which are prescribed by a specialist doctor. It is however recommended that all stress management techniques should be tried before going for medications as these tend to have lots of side effects on the body.

Therefore, stress causing-factors must be first identified and then, alleviated via particular techniques. This would not only help a person fight this menace but also can keep them fit and healthy for a longer period.

CHAPTER FOUR

How to Maximize Your Potential

We are all endowed with a special thing – our potential. Some of us realize this potential quite early in life, whereas, for some, it takes a lifetime to realize this. These latter people who take time to realize their potential often accept the fact that they have lost the time needed to bring their real potential to the surface. That is why it is really important to realize your potential within a given period, or else it's often too late to begin.

Moreover, one can also realize their hidden talent while discovering their real potential. This is done with experience, with the help of family, friends and even enemies. However, quite unfortunately, people at times also tend to de-motivate a person to such an extent that their search for their hidden potential becomes lost in their misery. That is why we recommend some general guidelines which can be adopted to buff and polish your hidden potential.

1. Read books: If you want to discover your hidden talent or potential, you can explore and search your interests and stay abreast of the latest happenings in your field of interest. This would not only keep you updated, but also make you flourish especially if your career is in your interest fields.

2. Expand your exposure: You need to expose yourself to different happenings that take place these days. In many cases, you will realize that your hidden potential lies in the knowledge that you were exposed to since childhood. So you must travel to places, research topics of interest and make social networks with associates that might help you discover your hidden potential.

3. Find a good mentor: A successful mentor who understands you would certainly make you realize your hidden potential. They will help you regarding matters such as dealing with family matters, business dealings and other aspects. A mentor would certainly bring about that hidden talent that you have not realized yet.

4. Take challenging work: Taking up challenges would help you optimize your potential and find it. Being out of your comfort zone would not only make you realize what you are made of, but you would also be surprised to discover those aspects of your personality that are unknown to you.

5. Participate in competitions: Participating in competitions would help you tap into your talent pool and discover the undiscovered! This would need you to maximize your time and energy and enhance your skills.

6. Try new things: You should treat every day as a new day, a new beginning. Look ahead at new avenues and don't hesitate to try new things or take risks.

Every one of us has unique potential hidden inside us. All we need to do is to wake up and start looking for them.

Overcoming Self-Limiting Beliefs

Life is difficult. We tend to face problems and hurdles at every phase of our life. Yet, we know that we have to look ahead and pace up. The hurdles can be in the form of family conflicts, financial problems, health-related issues or problems related to adjustment in social life. All of these are related to the self-limiting beliefs that stop us from moving ahead.

The basis of this issue is that the smallest perception can create a belief that gradually grows larger. A lot of times, we tend to become unconscious and tend to direct all our actions by these self-formed beliefs. These subconscious acts tend to slowly become a part of our character and result in a huge impact on our personality. When we talk about such beliefs, these can be of various types. There are many beliefs which tend to have a positive impact on our personality and lifestyle. However, in some cases, these beliefs can be negative, which when reinforced in our personality, tend to create a huge impact and makes us weak.

When facing such obstacles in life, one has to always deal with perseverance and courage. The stronger we face these obstacles, the lesser they'll become. There are also other ways to deal with these obstacles such as the following:

1. **Positive thinking:** This is the first step towards clearing your obstacles. The very thought of quitting a task would never let you succeed at all. That is why a positive frame of mind is needed at all times to find a solution to the problems and obstacles you face. Positive thinking not only lets you have clear thinking but also makes you focus on what you want to achieve.

2. **Relax your mind:** Tension and stress would never let you succeed in life. Being tension-free would make you

focus so that a good number of obstacles are eliminated.

3. Perseverance and persistence: The problem would not solve on its own. But you need to wait for the results to surface. This patience and endurance is an experience in itself, which, through the test of time, would make you a whole new insight into the notion of the problem.

4. Find new opportunities: Dynamism is the key to success. So don't wait for opportunities to show up. Rather, take charge and find new challenges and opportunities in your daily routine work. It would not only make you creative but would give you lots of determination and strength.

5. Inspiration: The element of inspiration is the wish or dream that makes you work harder and overcome obstacles. Inspiration gives the spark that one needs to propel ahead towards a higher future.

CHAPTER FIVE

Aspects of Human Behaviour to Succeed

Motivation is the reason which instils people to embark upon certain behaviour that is persuasive. This persuasive nature tends to motivate people towards that particular task, goal or objective. Therefore, motivation is the force that drives an individual and propels them towards their objectives.

To be motivated, one has to adapt to certain behavioural patterns that bring the mind to work dynamically. Therefore, it is a state of mind which is not related to one's personality but is rather adopted by an intrinsically motivated person. Certain aspects of behaviours tend to propel a person towards being motivated. These are Arousal of behaviour, Direction of behaviour and Persistence of behaviour.

1) Arousal of behaviour:

This is the triggering factor that brings a change of mind. When a person is motivated, he or she tends to start thinking about the actions related to what motivated them. These actions arouse one's behaviour in which certain action plans are created in the mind of the motivated person. Therefore, arousal is also the activation of behaviour.

2) Direction of behaviour:

The direction of behaviour is the alignment of one's thoughts and action plans so that a sense of direction is formed. When a person's behaviours are directed, he or she tends to maintain their focus towards their target objective. Moreover, the direction also maintains one's thoughts towards that particular action plan.

3) Persistence of behaviour:

Persistence is an important element in motivation as it ensures continuity and concreteness regarding the action plans. It also maintains one's motivation and continues the goal achievement of the person.

Other than these behavioural aspects, motivation is also catered by some important motives. These can be psychological or physiological which fall under Homeostatic motives (such as those important for living, for example, thirst, hunger, etc.); Non-homeostatic motives (such as shelter-seeking habits, curiosity, etc.) and Social/ Learned motives (such as approval, appreciation, etc.).

Homeostatic elements are inborn and need not be nurtured as such. They are present as an inherent part of one's nature. Non-homeostatic elements tend to be affected by the surroundings and can arise due to general observation. However, social or learned motives are different in every individual as people tend to behave differently, face a variety of situations and are shaped continuously by the people and the situation they face. That is why every individual's response to these motives is quite different, depending on their upbringing, experience and learning pattern. Therefore, every individual responds differently when motivated, which is exhibited via the behavioural aspects and individual motives. The key point to note here is that no matter how you are conditioned, always respond positively to maximize your potential and harbour your motivation.

Once you learn how to control these behavioural aspects, you can take charge of yourself and change sails according to the direction your life propels you in. This would make you move easily into the realms of success.

The Role of Education

Education is one of the fundamental principles on which one's success depends. To understand the role of education and its impact on success, one has to first understand how one measures a successful life. A successful life can be denominated by a person's wealth, fame, career position, property, assets and most of all, personality. While many argue that one needs to have luck for success and those who are born with wealth and assets are already successful, we do need to realize that being born with assets would not make us successful until we prove ourselves to be worthy of it.

So regardless of the fact whether you are born rich or poor, you need to focus on how you can be successful and how you can maintain this position of yours. Now comes the question, why do people press on being educated to be successful? Well, it's quite simple. Education gives you the sense of direction, the knowledge, the skills and the focus which is needed to be successful. Of course, a good rationale is also important as many who have succeeded in their career paths have done so because they made good decisions. But our decisions eventually depend on our education and are in some way affected by our level of education and experience.

An educated entrepreneur and an uneducated entrepreneur have different approaches, strategies and planning tendencies. Moreover, education makes you stand out amongst the others and gives you dignity and grace. The chances of having better-paid jobs and even better careers are all dependent on your level of education. College dropouts such as Bill Gates – Microsoft, Michael Cell – Dell computers and Steve Jobs of Apple are some of the exceptions who were either so intelligent or hardworking that lack of education didn't stop them to be successful. But following their path is not everybody's rule of the game as we have to face the reality rather than dream about exceptions. Despite not having a college degree, these men were so hardworking and intelligent, that they are today's billionaires. However, not everybody can follow in the footsteps of these exceptional men as we don't have the required intelligence or the luck to make it as big as they are. So, what exactly do we do to make it as big? We can't just sit down and start dreaming.

The best thing to do in these circumstances is to take charge and get educated. A Masters or any Professional degree is the key to success as these degrees would not only land us in better-paying jobs but also make us worthy of them. Our personality and values would be shaped by the education we get, which would help us to deal with the numerous business and corporate situations that otherwise leave us confused. Moreover, our inner-self would also be strengthened via education as the values that our education would give us would also help us to portray ourselves in a much better way to society.

So always remember, the key to success is good education as it transforms our knowledge, values and our approach towards the way to success.

CHAPTER SIX

Social Roles for a Successful Life

Having a great friend circle and socializing with people is a great way to propel your life ahead. It's not always that we come across people whom we get on well with. However, having an active social life is a great way to keep you boosted. Spending time with people not only makes your moods uplifted but also enhances your emotional well-being, personality and manners. The key point to understand here is that one should not only make a lot of friends but rather, be friends with those people who are open-minded and ambitious. Such positive people tend to have a lot of positive influence on your life.

However, while making social connections, we must realize some social habits that would be toxic for our social relations and should be best avoided. In this regard, some of the following tips should be implemented while socializing with an open-minded social circle:

1. Talk about the motivation and passion of others:

A good social asset for all times is to talk about the social assets of others as much as you can. This would make you find out what inspires them and how they tend to be so intrinsically motivated. You can discuss their passions and ask them why they are so attracted towards them. As you get better at this skill, you will realize that at times, you can even discover somebody's hidden potential that even they are unaware of.

2. Don't whine:

Whining is a major push-away. It's a highly negative sign, a red alert for those whom you socialize with. Moreover, it makes your social circle dislike you. So get away from this whining habit. Even though you might think that you don't whine, people around you might be more sensitive about this issue. Just be more self-conscious to realize how much people around you suffer from your whining and how often you do it! Do understand that complaint and whining are two different things. You complain when you calmly elaborate on how something is unacceptable and how it should change. However, whining is a different scenario.

3. Don't boast:

Boasting might give us great happiness, and boost the ego for a bit, but tends to be quite detrimental to our social life. However, nobody prefers to be in the company of a boaster and it often leaves a bad impression on the people you socialize with. Only if you are a comedian and are boasting for fun, then it is sure to be taken in a light-hearted manner.

However, you also need to have a distinction between honesty and boasting. If you are honestly telling others about your achievements, then there is no need for you to hide them. Rather, if you feel like telling others about something, then that is supposed to be boasting.

So evaluate yourself on these parameters and try to judge yourself about where you go wrong while socializing with people. Correct yourself and use these tips to properly interact with people and move towards a positive personal change.

What Makes a Person Unsuccessful

There have been many articles written on how to be successful, but very few of them cite the factors that make you unsuccessful! To be successful, there are certain factors that you have to avoid to ensure success. Some of these elements are:

1. **False beliefs:** Any incorrect idea that you have about something is a false belief. The best element for success is to let go of false beliefs by getting over them and moving ahead. A small false belief such as being unlucky or not able to find a job should not stop you from looking for a job. To get over false beliefs, one has to get out of their comfort zone and accept challenges so that one can overcome false beliefs and move on towards newer horizons.

2. **External control:** A particular way of thinking which is strongly associated with being unsuccessful is blaming everything on external factors. For instance, when one doesn't perform well in an examination, they blame their teacher or the environment around them. Whereas, successful people revert to their internal locus of control where they believe that they are in control of everything. They strengthen themselves internally so that they can face whatever challenges life throws at them.

3. **Persistence and perseverance:** Successful people tend to be persistent in life. They tend to continue their hard work until they achieve what they want. Losing hope

quickly is a sign of unsuccessful people who don't stand up after they fail. So be strong and persistent if you wish to succeed.

4. **Rigidity:** Unsuccessful people are quite rigid. They tend to stick to their obsolete ways and do not like adapting to changing situations. In this dynamic world, one needs to be highly flexible to be successful. You need to adapt to situations accordingly, take hardships and try different methods if you fail.

5. **Improper planning:** Being planned for your future would guarantee you success. If you have your plans, you will maintain your focus and head in the correct direction. Those who are unsuccessful do not plan or even if they do, their plans are incomplete. Therefore, you need to be planned else you'll be swept by those around you.

6. **Lack of self-confidence:** Ever wondered why the unsuccessful ones are always left behind? It's all because they lack the confidence of presenting their ideas in front of their bosses. You should speak up, be creative and give ideas so that the people around you realize that you are confident.

7. **Reminiscing about lack of resources:** A lot of unsuccessful ones stay behind just because they think that they don't have the money or the resources to do things. Why stay behind? If you are affirmative that you have to be successful, you'll have to do things without resources.

8. **Fears:** These are not the fears of the dark or the height, but rather these are the fears which hinder your ability to leap ahead towards success. Although the opposite, the fear of success or failure can both hinder your way towards being successful so overcome your fears and

start moving ahead!

Criteria for idealizing successful people

We, as individuals, have lots of aspirations and dreams. Throughout stage of growing up, we tend to idealize key people in our life, who can either be our favourite movie stars, sportsmen, teachers, family members or even politicians. This gradual idealism leaves an impact on us and at times, our personality reflects certain traits of our ideals which we have absorbed from them over time.

So is there a certain criterion for idealizing people in our life? Should we randomly idealize just anybody who inspires us? Well, the thing is that not all individuals are worthy of idealism. It also depends upon how, we, as individuals, would want to see ourselves. A thief would always idealize his mafia leader, not the local priest! So, if we aspire to be worthy and successful individuals, then we need to idealize people who have the following important traits:

- **Positive attitude:** A positive attitude not only makes us successful but also makes us open to all the opportunities that come our way. Successful people have positivity radiating from them and they never let go of any opportunity. It is these minute opportunities that have made them climb their success ladders.
- **Value time:** Successful people also value their time. They are well-prioritized and planned for the day. Not only that, but they also value the time of others and fulfil their deadlines accordingly. When going to a meeting, they are always on time and well-planned.

- **Accountability:** Despite being high-risk takers, successful people tend to be accountable for their actions, successes and failures. They do not blame their environment or the people, just in case any plan fails.
- **Proactive:** Being well-planned is the key trait of successful people. They are proactive in their actions and their positive attitude supports their proactive measures.
- **Creative:** Creativity is the key to success. Creativity lets you see new opportunities and work towards them. All leaders are supposed to be creative as their creativity makes them implement certain changes that are required for a total turnover of an organization's pace.
- **Well-communicated:** Good communication skills are an important asset for successful individuals. Being well-versed not only in verbal but also non-verbal communication skills reflects hugely upon the personality of a successful individual. Reaching out to others via communication can attract a lot of people towards you who may also bring newer opportunities.
- **Resilience:** Being successful is not a piece of cake. It takes a lot of perseverance and resilience as successes do not come without failures. The strength needed to stand up after failing is the actual test that successful people go through. This means that resilience, as a trait, should never be overlooked while selecting successful ideals. A person cannot be successful if they haven't undergone any offsets.

Above mentioned traits are amongst the few traits that successful people have. However, these traits are quite worthy and one can look for these traits while selecting their ideals.

Maintaining a Work-Life Balance

The world is changing so rapidly that every other person now has to work to live a better life. In this race, one often tends to mix up their personal and professional life. This results in a jumbled up life, messed up priorities, lack of time and overall dissatisfaction. This also gives a feeling to the person that despite all the hard work, one has still something missing in life. This missing element is the mental peace and tranquillity that one needs to concentrate on in life.

It is therefore advisable that one follows certain rules to keep their lives simple and live a healthier life with a balance between the personal and professional life. Some of these factors are in your control whereas some may be out of the domains of your control. For convenience, we'll look at some tips which are divided into three aspects below:

At work:

1) Take small breaks during the day. A ten-minute break can be taken every two hours so that your effectiveness and work productivity can be enhanced.

2) Prioritize your day and divide your time realistically.

3) Limit all email correspondence to the office only. Don't take your pending work home.

4) Distinction between the work and personal life should be kept separate. Don't work or think about work 24/7.

5) Deal with unrealistic deadlines before it is too late. Communicate the problems to your boss to avoid issues at the last moment.

6) Go on vacations so you can return fresh at work.

At home:

1) Relax and spend time with family after returning from work.

2) Divide household chores amongst family members so that after all the work is completed, the family can sit together and share some quality time.

3) Exercise even for at least 10 minutes a day. It would refresh you and you'll feel more energized.

4) Eat healthy food so that you have the energy to spend time with your family and also to work productively.

5) Adopt a hobby that you can pursue with your family or friends. This would keep your mind off work and also make you much more energized. Hobbies are also quite effective to alleviate stress so you can use a good hobby and make use of it.

In community:

1) Spend some quality time in your community. Devote some voluntary time to community work so that you can devote your money, education and time to social work. This would enhance your satisfaction level and also bring you a sense of social responsibility. You can also generate funds, help in arranging corporate social responsibilities and use your maximum capacity to serve your community.

2) You can also participate in your children's school events and parental societies to know what your child is learning at school. Parental groups are also involved in organizing functions and social tasks for school children. This would not only help you manage your time, but also inculcate such social and extracurricular habits in your children.

CHAPTER EIGHT

Dealing with Life Challenges

It is quite well known to all that everything starts from our mind. The smallest thought is generated into an idea, which takes the shape of the actions to be implemented. This whole process is being functioned within one's mind so that one can plan. That is why positivity is an important thinking approach that all successful people have. We have all been generously granted positivity inside us, but then again, it's a matter of choice for those who want to use it or not. People who are positive in their approaches seem to attract us more than those who are negative and always blame things or their environment for the mishaps.

Our thought processes are controlled by our mind which also reflects and is exhibited by our behaviour, attitude and perception. It also shows the type of lifestyle we would prefer. Those who are happy tend to have positive thinking which radiates around them. However, those who are gloomy have a negative aura that radiates around them. Therefore, it is up to us as to what type of lifestyle we prefer. Happiness and misery, both are important elements of life. No matter how rich one is, one can certainly never avoid happiness or misery. These problems which envelop us tend to make us stronger internally as they teach us about life, values and how to face different challenges that we come across in our daily routine. It is generally seen that those people who face their life challenges positively have positive results whereas those who face challenges with a negative attitude usually end up with a negative result. So what exactly should your approach be while facing life challenges?

Below are some tips which will guide you to improve your daily routine and build upon your inner self:

1. When facing negative thoughts, try to change them into positive ones. Always remember that you can control your thoughts, your thoughts shouldn't control the way you live! So instead of complaining and blaming others, evaluate your options. Think of the best possible solution under the given circumstances and act upon them

2. Don't hang out with negative people. Rather, stay in the company of those who think positively. Talk or get counselling with people who tend to think positively and are a source of inspiration for you.

3. Find happiness in the simple things in life. Remember to look upon the less fortunate and be thankful for what you have.

4. Love yourself instead of blaming. Be kind and respect others. Do small gestures of kindness such as a simple smile and hello to the watchman, helping the elderly, etc. The positive signals you send out are met with positivity in response which increases your satisfaction level.

5. Help the unfortunate people. Give some voluntary service at an orphan shelter or a nursing home. Spend

time with the miserable and radiate your positivity onto them.

Always remember, you get what you give. So always send signals of positivity and give hope to others. Do remember that when you give others a reason to smile for and hope to cherish, you'll also get that back manifold.